HEALTH

IS

WEALTH

by

DR. VERONIA `LANI B. DECENA-MAGAT

COPYRIGHT HEALTH IS WEALTH

By Veronia `Lani B. Decena Magat

ISBN:

Hardbound-978-621-470-751-5

Softbound/Paperback-978-621-470-752-2

PDF (downloadable)-978-621-470-753-9

Published by:

Poetry Planet Book Publishing House

Rosario, Pozorrubio, Pangasinan, Philippines

Contact Number: 09554960094

Email: maritesritumalta@gmail.com

DEDICATION

Thank you, Lord Jesus Christ, for giving me the inspiration and insight to write this book. I also want to thank my family, especially my husband, and son, for being there for me and supporting me no matter what. Thank you to my family, who has always supported me in my endeavors. To my closest companion, who has always been there for me. And to everyone who values health and wellness, may this book serve as motivation to take a more holistic approach to life. Let us all strive for a future where everyone has access to good healthcare and where we may all enjoy the company of those we care about.

PREFACE

The necessity of caring for one's physical, mental, and emotional health is explored at length in Health is Wealth, a comprehensive guide to healthy living. Adopting a healthy lifestyle and making mindful decisions for our well-being are of the utmost significance in today's fast-paced and stressful society. This book is a valuable and informative resource that discusses many facets of wellness, from diet and exercise to stress reduction and emotional well-being. Health is Wealth teaches its readers how to take charge of their health and reach peak wellness using concrete examples and doable recommendations. This book is a must-read for anybody interested in increasing their quality of life and achieving true wealth: the wealth of good health.

TABLE OF CONTETS

Chapter 1

CONCEPT OF HEALTH

"True health and wealth are not found in material possessions or external validation, but in the simple joys of a wholesome life filled with love, connection, and fulfillment."

The adage that "health is wealth" serves to stress the value of physical and mental wellness is universally acknowledged. This idiom implies that one's physical and psychological well-being are equally important forms of riches. Good health is the cornerstone around which we may build our entire lives; while many associate riches with material belongings or financial assets, this is not the case.

One's state of health is paramount. Improving a high fitness level increases one's quality of life by facilitating their ability to engage in mental and physical activities. It allows us to perform at a high level in our jobs, spend quality time with our loved ones, and enjoy our favorite pastimes. When we're physically and mentally fit, we can take in all that life has to offer. However, when our health is poor, it might hinder our performance and negatively affect our state of mind and body.

But the value of health extends far beyond our individual lives. A prosperous, productive, and functional society is a healthy society. A nation's (and a community's) health is crucial to its economic development and survival. The absence of sick people from the labor force hurts economic growth and productivity. Furthermore, health issues might result in high healthcare expenses before denying the person and society.

The idea that health is wealth also highlights the importance of preventative health care. It implies that spending money on one's health is a good idea because it can reduce the need for medical treatment and its associated expenses. Prevention is the key to better health, which means working out regularly, eating right, and getting enough sleep.

When you take care of your health, you lower your chances of developing severe conditions like diabetes, heart disease, and stroke. Worldwide, chronic diseases are the primary cause of mortality and disability, and they are becoming more common in modern culture. They also play a significant role in driving up the price of medical care.

Taking care of our physical health can have a positive effect on our minds as well. A healthy physique can help maintain a sense of and vice versa. Exercising has been linked to better mood, sharper thinking, and less stress and anxiety.

But in today's hectic and stressful environment, it's not always easy to maintain a healthy lifestyle. A person's health status can be affected by several factors, including their environment, genetics, and access to medical care. Preventative care and lifestyle decisions that improve health and longevity are paramount. Altering one's immediate surroundings for the better and expanding one's access to quality medical treatment are two more factors that can improve health outcomes.

The idea that health is wealth highlights how important it is to care for one's health on a personal, community, and societal level. Putting our health first allows us to avoid being sick, save money on medical treatment, and increase our quality of life. The time and effort put into maintaining a healthy lifestyle is time and effort well spent, with personal and societal rewards. Realizing the importance of our health and taking preventative measures to ensure it remains at a high level throughout our lives is crucial.

Importance of Health to Teens and Adults

"A healthy body and clear mind are priceless presents. Living a healthy lifestyle takes effort, but it pays off in the long run, both physically and monetarily."

The state of one's health is a significant component in determining one's happiness at any age. Poor lifestyle decisions often cause obesity, cardiovascular disease, diabetes, and other serious health issues. Even though today's youth often feels unstoppable, it's never too early to start making the kind of healthful decisions that will benefit them for the rest of their life. Adults need to prioritize their health because of the stress and poor habits that can result from leading a busy life. In this piece, we'll examine several factors that make fitness crucial at any age.

The value of health in adults and adolescents extends much beyond that of mere survival. A deterioration in health can have adverse effects on one's career, relationships, and bank account. However, a healthy body is essential for a fulfilling existence. Being in excellent health is vital to enjoying life and participating in sightseeing, making new friends, and developing interests. A person's mental and emotional well-being might benefit from hobbies and social activities, as well.

Teens and adults alike should prioritize their own physical and mental wellness. Some of the most important things a person can do for their health are to eat well, get plenty of sleep, exercise regularly, deal with stress, and ask for help when needed. Chronic diseases, mental health problems, and financial and social difficulties are only some outcomes that could result from ignoring one's health. Boosting one's quality of life is possible through preventive care, self-care, and social support. Taking care of one's health ensures happiness and success in the here and now and in the future.

As we age, maintaining our health becomes crucial to maintaining our standard of living. Avoiding future health hazards and maintaining a healthy lifestyle requires kids and adults to put their physical, mental, and emotional health first. The importance of maintaining good health cannot be overstated, and this is true for both young people and adults.

Condition of the body:

All people, regardless of age, should prioritize maintaining a healthy body. When your body is healthy, you may go about your everyday routine without worrying about getting hurt or damaging your health. Teenagers' bodies are still maturing, so taking care of their physical well-being is crucial. For healthy growth and development, they need to eat well, exercise, and get plenty of shut-eye. However, adults should keep their bodies in good shape to forestall the onset of age-related conditions, including diabetes, hypertension, and cardiovascular disease.

Mental Illness:

The condition of one's mind is just as crucial as that of one's body. The ability to manage one's feelings, deal with adversity, and create positive bonds with others is part of this. Anxiety, depression, and stress are all mental health conditions that can afflict anyone at any time. However, due to the difficulties of life transitions, interpersonal interactions, peer pressure, and other age-specific stresses, adolescents, and adults are at a higher risk for developing these mental health problems. Both groups need good mental health to participate fully in society, form satisfying relationships, and realize their ambitions.

Emotional well-being:

To maintain emotional health, one must be in tune with and able to communicate their feelings appropriately. Empathy, self-awareness, and elevated self-esteem are positive traits that can develop from maintaining a balanced emotional state. Adolescents' emotional well-being is essential to their social and intellectual development. Similarly, when grown-ups emphasize their emotional well-being, they reap the rewards of less stress, better interpersonal connections, and a fuller sense of purpose in life.

Future health risk prevention:

If you put your health first today, you won't have to worry about it afterward. Teenagers can benefit from this by developing positive routines and understanding the significance of self-care. The best way for an adult to avoid creating a chronic disease and age gracefully is to practice good preventive health habits. Checkups once a year, a healthy diet, frequent exercise, and stress reduction are all excellent examples.

Improved well-being:

Above all else, taking care of one's health should be your top priority. Adolescents can benefit from this by having a more satisfying experience and establishing lifelong healthy routines. Adults who put their health first often have fewer health problems and a more satisfying existence.

In summary, maintaining good health is essential for people of all ages. Taking care of your body, mind, and spirit can have far-reaching positive effects on your life, including increased efficiency, improved confidence, and overall happiness. It's never too early or too late to start prioritizing health because doing so can avert future health issues. The future is brighter and healthier if you put money into your health now.

Chapter 2

PHYSICAL HEALTH

"The greatest reward for the money you put into yourself is a long and healthy life."

You can't put too much emphasis on taking care of your body. It's crucial to us and has far-reaching effects on our daily lives. To be in good physical health means to be in a condition where everyday activities pose no difficulties. It is the basis of a happy life and optimal mental and physical health.

Our cardiovascular and muscular systems, our respiratory and reproductive systems, our digestive and immunological systems, and our digestive and gastrointestinal tracts are all part of our physical health. All of these systems work together to maintain our health, and they respond favorably to the attention we give them.

The immune system, which protects us from bacteria, viruses, and other ailments, receives a significant boost when our bodies are in good shape. The immune system is an intricate system of cells and molecules that cooperate to maintain our good health. Regular exercise, a nutritious diet, and sufficient sleep contribute to a more robust immune system and a healthier body.

Maintaining a healthy body also has positive effects on our minds. Physical activity has been demonstrated to improve mental health by lowering stress, increasing confidence, and easing the symptoms of sadness and anxiety. Exercising releases endorphins (feel-good chemicals) and decreases cortisol (stress hormone), resulting in an overall sense of well-being and peace of mind.

Enhancing our mental capacities is also aided by taking care of our bodies. Exercising frequently improves cognitive abilities like memory, focus, and problem-solving. It also helps the brain perform better and protects against mental deterioration as we age. Maintaining a healthy brain also requires eating a balanced diet full of foods rich in the vitamins and minerals the brain needs.

Having a healthy body is about more than just eating right. Many serious health issues, including diabetes, heart disease, and stroke, have been linked to obesity. Preventing and controlling these diseases with a healthy lifestyle can lengthen your life and lower your chance of problems.

Chronic disorders, including high blood pressure, heart disease, and cancer, are all made worse by inactivity. In contrast, regular exercise has been shown to minimize the danger of cardiovascular disease and some malignancies. The risk of bone and joint infections, including osteoporosis and arthritis, can be reduced by regular physical activity.

Living a healthy and fulfilling life requires a combination of various factors, including daily exercise, proper diet and nutrition, and adequate rest, sleep, and recreation. These three elements serve as the foundation for optimal health and well-being. In this article, we will explore the benefits and importance of each of these factors.

Daily Exercise:

1. Reduces the risk of chronic diseases such as heart disease, stroke, and diabetes.
2. Improves cardiovascular health and promotes healthy blood flow.
3. Helps maintain healthy body weight and body mass index (BMI).
4. Boosts mood and improves mental health by increasing endorphins.
5. Enhances immune function and reduces the risk of infections.
6. Increases bone density and reduces the risk of osteoporosis.
7. Improves flexibility, balance, and coordination.
8. Enhances cognitive function and brain health.
9. Promotes better sleep and reduces the risk of sleep disorders.
10. Increases lifespan and improves the overall quality of life.

Proper Diet and Nutrition:

1. Provides essential nutrients that the body needs to function correctly.
2. Supports healthy growth and development in children and adolescents.
3. Helps maintain healthy body weight and BMI.
4. Reduces the risk of chronic diseases such as heart disease, stroke, and cancer.

5. Boosts immune function and reduces the risk of infections.
6. Improves energy levels and reduces fatigue.
7. Supports healthy digestion and gut health.
8. Helps regulate blood sugar levels and reduces the risk of diabetes.
9. Promotes healthy skin, hair, and nails.
10. Improves mental health and cognitive function.

Enough Rest, Sleep, and Recreation:

1. Reduces the risk of chronic diseases such as heart disease, stroke, and obesity.
2. Improves cognitive function and mental health.
3. Boosts immune function and reduces the risk of infections.
4. Promotes healthy digestion and gut health.
5. Enhances physical performance and reduces the risk of injury.
6. Increases lifespan and improves the overall quality of life.
7. Reduces stress and improves mood.
8. Helps regulate hormone levels and reduces the risk of hormonal imbalances.
9. Improves cardiovascular health and promotes healthy blood flow.
10. Promotes better sleep and reduces the risk of sleep disorders.

Daily exercise, proper diet and nutrition, and enough rest, sleep, and recreation are all essential factors for optimal health and well-being. By prioritizing these elements and making them a part of your daily routine, you can improve your overall health, reduce your risk of chronic diseases, and enhance your quality of life.

Here are ten tips for maintaining good Mental Health

PHYSICAL HEALTH

Good physical health is vitally important for our overall well-being, but many of us don't take proper steps toward ensuring it. Making small changes to your everyday lifestyle can go a long way to help you maintain good physical health and lead a healthier life. Here are ten tips to help you stay physically healthy:

1. **Exercise regularly**: Abundant scientific evidence indicates that exercise can help maintain physical and mental health. Get at least 30 minutes of moderate exercise daily, such as aerobic, strength training, and flexibility exercises.

2. **Eat a well-balanced diet:** Get plenty of fresh fruits and vegetables in your daily diet. Avoid processed foods as much as possible, as they are usually high in sugar and fat.

3. **Drink plenty of water:** Staying hydrated is critical to maintaining good physical health. Drink at least eight glasses of water daily to keep your body functioning correctly.

4. **Get quality sleep:** Get at least seven to eight hours each night. Experts recommend avoiding caffeine or alcohol in the evenings and establishing a regular sleep schedule.

5. **Avoid smoking and excessive alcohol**: Tobacco and alcohol consumption has been linked with several adverse health effects, including heart problems and

cancer. It is best to avoid these substances as much as possible.

6. **Practice mindful eating:** Eat meals regularly and leisurely. Eating quickly can be linked with overeating and other digestive problems. It's important to foster healthy eating habits to maintain good physical health.

7. **Practice good hygiene:** Shower regularly, brush your teeth twice a day, and wear clean clothes each day. Proper hygiene can help you avoid getting sick and enhance your overall well-being.

8. **Reduce stress:** Stress can negatively impact physical health. Take a break from work or school if things become overwhelming. Unwind with a relaxing activity such as yoga, walking, or reading.

9. **Get regular medical check-ups:** Regular medical check-ups can help catch any potential health problems early before they become more serious. Make sure to get routine physicals and get any recommended screenings and immunizations.

10. **Connect with family and friends:** Take the time to connect with friends and family. Social interaction can reduce stress and improve mental health.

By following these steps, you can help ensure your physical health is in tip-top shape. Remember that physical health goes hand-in-hand with mental health, as both are important for a healthy, balanced lifestyle.

"The Benefits of Detoxification"
(Cleanse Your Body and Mind)

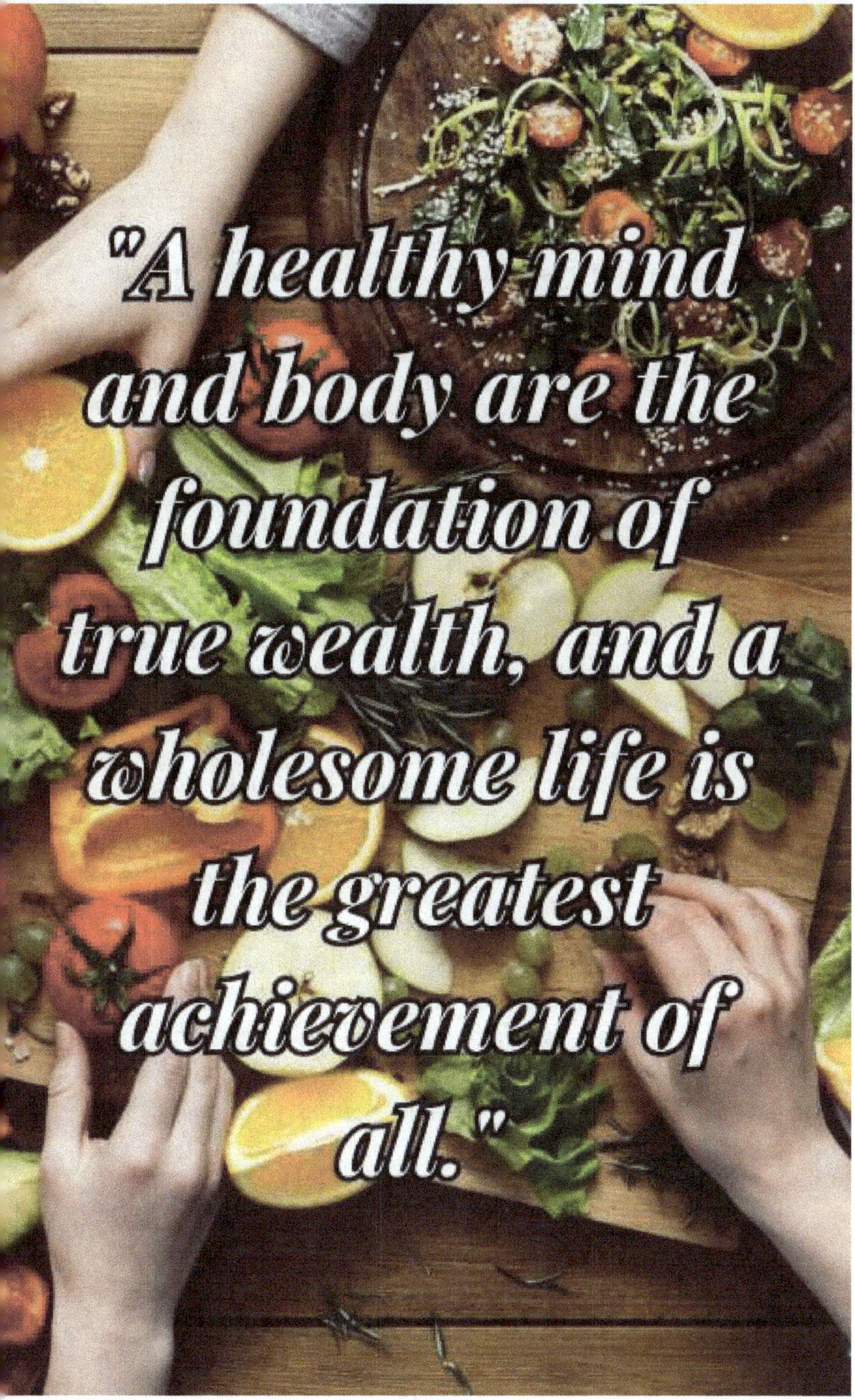

"A healthy mind and body are the foundation of true wealth, and a wholesome life is the greatest achievement of all."

In the last several years, detoxification has become a popular topic, especially in health and wellness. Detoxification eliminates harmful substances from one's physical form, mental state, and spiritual being. Pollutants in the air, water, and soil; lousy food; stress; and unpleasant mental and emotional states all contribute to this poisoning. Detoxification aims to improve health by eliminating harmful substances. This essay will discuss the merits of detoxification and offer advice on cleansing your physical body, mental state, and spiritual self.

Physical Detoxification

Toxins enter our systems in countless ways, including the air we breathe, the food we eat, and the things we use. Long-term exposure to these pollutants can cause digestive troubles, headaches, exhaustion, and even chronic disease. Eliminating these poisons through detoxification can help the body operate more smoothly and effectively.

Detoxing through food is one of the most effective methods. Fruits, vegetables, whole grains, and lean proteins are all great examples of whole, unprocessed foods that aid in the body's natural detoxification processes. Water helps the body wash out impurities and maintain normal functioning, so drinking enough is essential.

Physical activity is another strategy for facilitating detoxification. Increasing your heart rate and sweating it out regularly will help eliminate harmful pollutants more efficiently. In particular, the physical activity and deep breathing that makeup yoga can aid in treating digestive and circulatory issues.

Detoxification by methods such as dry brushing, saunas, and hydrotherapy is another option. The practice of dry brushing involves using a brush made of natural bristles to exfoliate the skin and activate the lymphatic system. Detoxification can also be aided by improving circulation and enhancing the body's biological detoxification processes using saunas and hydrotherapy, such as hot and cold showers.

Mental Detoxification

Detoxing the mind is equally as vital as cleansing the body. Constant exposure to stress, negative thoughts, and emotions can devastate our emotional and psychological well-being. Taking mental hygiene measures can positively affect one's stress levels, disposition, and level of concentration.

Mindfulness meditation is a powerful tool for mental hygiene. Meditation entails paying attention to the here and now without evaluating it or letting thoughts wander. This can bring inner peace and tranquility, relieving tension, anxiety, and depression.

Journaling is another tool for mental hygiene. Putting your thoughts and feelings on paper can be a cathartic experience that helps you gain perspective. Positive emotions and decreased stress levels can also result from practicing gratitude or thinking about what you must be grateful for.

Purification of the Spirit

Finally, when it comes to detoxification, it's crucial to keep the soul in mind. The soul is the center of our being as human beings, and it needs the same kind of attention and nourishment as our physical and mental selves. The soul can be cleansed through spiritual practices such as prayer, going to mass, spiritual reading, and exercise. This is helping us to rediscover our true selves and the significance of our existence.

Mindfulness meditation with a spiritual focus can be an effective means of purifying the spirit. Meditation is the practice of concentrating one's thoughts on our faith to achieve a state of calm and harmony within oneself.

Spending time in nature is another approach to purifying the spirit. Inspiring awe and wonder, which can lead to personal development and a stronger sense of belonging to a broader whole, is one of nature's many gifts to us.

Finally, taking care of yourself might help you purify your spirit. This could be anything from having a hot bath or performing yoga to hanging out with friends and family.

Overall, the benefits of detoxification to one's health and well-being cannot be overstated. Stress is reduced, mental clarity is enhanced, and a connection to one's inner self is facilitated through physical, mental, and spiritual detoxification. Detoxification can be encouraged, and our quality of life can be improved by integrating diet, exercise, meditation, and spirituality.

15 Detoxification Hacks and Tips

1. Drink a glass of warm lemon water first thing in the morning to jumpstart your digestive system and help your body cleanse.

2. Boost your digestive health and facilitate detoxification by eating more fiber-rich foods, including whole grains, fruits, vegetables, nuts, and seeds.

3. Organic foods are free of chemicals and pesticides that can interfere with your body's natural detoxification processes, so it's essential to eat them. Eat more but more plant base.

4. Use herbs and spices: Herbs and spices like turmeric, ginger, garlic, thyme, and oregano can be utilized in cooking or taken as supplements due to their cleansing characteristics. Ginger is good for lowering

sugar and for the kidney. Camomile tea and corn silk lower creatinine levels and some studies show it cures kidney failure.

5. Try intermittent fasting: This method, in which you consume all your food within a specific window each day, can aid detoxification and digestion.

6. Try dry brushing, which entails using a particular brush to exfoliate the skin and encourage detoxification by stimulating the lymphatic system.

7. Include breathing exercises; pranayama and other deep breathing practices can increase oxygen flow and promote detoxification.

8. Keep hydrated; doing so aids in detoxification by flushing toxins and waste from the system.

9. Take advantage of water treatment by alternating hot and cold showers or soaking in the hot tub to stimulate the lymphatic system and facilitate cleansing.

10. Get a good night's rest. Sleep aids detoxification by allowing the body to rebuild and rejuvenate itself. Eight hours of sleep is still advisable, and a nap in the afternoon matters.

1 1. Regular exercise improves the body's ability to flush toxins by increasing blood flow and oxygenation.

12. You may aid your body's natural detoxification processes by paying more attention to the tastes, smells, and textures of your food.

13. Supplements like probiotics, milk thistle, and dandelion root can aid in detoxification by supporting the liver and digestive system.

14. Spending time in nature has been shown to aid the detoxification process by decreasing stress and promoting emotions of serenity.

15 Make time for prayer and meditation. These practices can aid detoxification by lowering stress and fostering a sense of inner peace.

Chapter 3

MENTAL HEALTH

"Health is the wealth that fills your life with happiness, while the latter states that a wholesome life is the key that unlocks the door to your dreams and aspirations."

The state of one's mind is crucial to their overall health and happiness. Mental health is often underestimated and undervalued compared to physical health, even though it is equally important. A person's mental health is measured by how well they think, feel, and interact with others. Resilience is the capacity to deal effectively with adversity, sustain positive professional and personal relationships, and enjoy a rich and satisfying existence.

A person's physical health, social life, and ability to do daily tasks are all affected by their mental health to varying degrees. A person's happiness, productivity, and social interaction ability are all impacted when their mental health declines. Conditions as diverse as high blood pressure, diabetes, heart disease, and autoimmune disorders have all been linked to those with poor mental health.

As a result, it's crucial to give mental health the same amount of attention as physical health. It entails changing one's way of benefits to benefit one's mental health and getting support when needed. In this chapter, we'll discuss the significance of self-care and stress management, the urgency of addressing mental health difficulties and getting help, the advantages of regular meditation and mindfulness practice, and more.

Learning How Mental Health Affects Physical Wellness

A person's mental health affects their physical health, and vice versa; similarly, a person's physical health can cause or exacerbate mental health issues. Therefore, both the mind and the body must practice self-care. Mentally healthy people can better deal with challenges and keep their relationships on a soundtrack. However, psychological distress can manifest physically through headaches, inability to sleep, and gastrointestinal pain.

Self-Care and Stress Management: Why They're Crucial

Taking care of one's mental health involves several factors, not the least of which are self-care and stress management. Respect for one's own emotional and physical well-being is referred to as self-care. It entails making stress-relieving and health-enhancing pursuits a top priority. Many people's moods and states of mind deteriorate due to stress. Therefore, learning how to deal with stress effectively can benefit emotional well-being.

Taking care of oneself means sleeping enough, eating right, drinking enough water, exercising, and establishing limits. Relaxation techniques, such as music, baths, books, and time with loved ones, can help immensely.

Deep breathing, gradual muscle relaxation, yoga, and meditation are all examples of relaxation practices that can help manage stress. Reframing negative ideas and altering one's perspective are also effective stress management strategies. They can learn to manage their time better and set priorities so they don't get overwhelmed.

Taking Care of Your Mental Health and Looking for Support

Knowing when you're having mental health problems is the first step in receiving the care you need. Depression, anxiety, bipolar disorder, and schizophrenia are just a few of the most frequently encountered mental health issues. These mental health issues might have a variety of causes. As a result, it is crucial to get to the bottom of things and fix whatever is causing the problem.

Many struggle to get help for mental health issues because they experience shame or stigma. There's also the stigma that comes with admitting you need assistance. Nonetheless, it takes courage to prioritize one's mental health. Therapists, psychiatrists, and psychologists are all professionals that people can visit for help with mental health issues. Depending on the patient's condition, these professionals may prescribe therapy, medicine, or a mix.

Mindfulness and meditation training

Mindfulness focuses on the here and now without attaching any significance to it. Mindfulness entails paying attention to the here and now and taking stock of one's internal and external states. Mindfulness training has been shown to have beneficial effects on stress management, anxiety reduction, and general psychological well-being.

One such healthy habit that boosts psychological well-being is meditation. Concentration is the mental process of paying close attention to one thing at a time. Meditation is a great way to relax and unwind the mind. It's good for your mental health and helps you stay sunny.

Conclusion

Maintaining physical and mental health requires constant attention to one's mental health. A person's physical health, social life, and ability to do daily tasks are all affected by their mental health to varying degrees. This is why it's so essential for people to practice mindfulness and meditation, as well as other forms of self-care and stress management, and to seek professional help when needed. Doing so can help people find harmony and fulfillment in their lives, improving their quality of life.

Stress is the precursor of physical and mental health issues

Stress has been known to be a destroyer of health and a cause of many diseases since the dawn of medicine. Metabolic and autoimmune diseases are some of the most common yet least talked about conditions today that can be caused by excessive and intense stress. Chronic stress can cause various physical and mental illnesses, so it's essential to learn how to reduce the stress levels in your life to live a healthy life. Here are five tips to avoid stress and have a healthy life:

1. Regular exercise helps reduce stress and improve your overall mental and physical health. Physical activity releases endorphins which act as natural painkillers and can enhance mood.

2. Avoid unhealthy habits: Unhealthy habits such as smoking and drinking alcohol can increase stress levels and lead to other health problems. Instead, focus on healthy alternatives such as eating healthy foods, drinking plenty of water, and getting enough sleep.

3. Practice mindfulness: Mindfulness is being aware of and focusing on the present moment. It can help you increase your resilience to stress and reduce anxiety. You can practice mindfulness through meditation, yoga, or even simply taking a few deep breaths and reminding yourself to be in the present moment.

4. Take breaks during the day: It is essential to take regular intervals during the day to give yourself a chance to relax and reset. This does not have to be a long break; even just a few minutes away from work can help to relieve stress.

5. Connect with others: Fostering positive connections with friends, family, or colleagues can help alleviate stress and give you the support you need to better cope with stressful situations. Investing in meaningful relationships can also give you a sense of purpose and joy in life.

Overall, stress can have a significant negative impact on both mental and physical health. However, by following these tips, you can reduce stress and live a healthier life.

Here are ten tips for maintaining good Mental Health

MENTAL
HEALTH TIPS

1. Value yourself: Treat yourself with kindness and respect, and avoid self-criticism.

2. Take care of your body: Eat nutritious meals, exercise regularly, and get enough sleep.

3. Connect with others: Make social connections a priority, especially face-to-face interactions.

4. Give back: Helping others can give you a sense of purpose and boost your mood.

5. Learn how to manage stress: Practice relaxation techniques, such as meditation, breathing exercises, or Zumba.

6. Practice gratitude: Remind yourself of things you are grateful for and focus on positivity.

7. Try something new: Experiment with a new hobby or activity to challenge yourself and boost creativity.

8. Laugh and have fun: Spend time with friends and family, watch a comedy, or try a fun activity.

9. Seek help when needed: Don't hesitate to seek professional assistance if you struggle with your mental health.

10. Take care of your brain: Eat foods rich in omega-3 fatty acids, which are linked to decreased rates of depression and schizophrenia.

Remember, maintaining good mental health is a journey, not a destination. Incorporating these tips into your daily routine can help you build resilience and improve your overall well-being.

Chapter 4

EMOTIONAL HEALTH

"Maintaining a healthy way of life is similar to caring for a valuable possession: it needs time, energy, and attention. Without it, we miss out on the best opportunities for happiness and prosperity that life has to offer."

A Guide to Recognizing Emotions and Taking Control of Your Life,

Feelings are fundamental to being human. They facilitate communication, friendship-building, and problem-solving. However, emotions can sometimes be challenging to control, and people often need help. To maintain emotional health, one must learn to recognize and cope with negative emotions healthily.

This chapter will go into greater detail on the subject of mental wellness. We'll talk about why it's so crucial to recognize and control your feelings. Emotional well-being also includes the development of emotional resilience and the maintenance of supportive connections at home and in the community. Last, we'll talk about some proven methods for handling adversity.

Feelings and Their Meanings

Emotions result from a multifaceted interaction between the mind and the body in reaction to external stimuli. Whether favorable or unfavorable, they can range from subtle to dramatic. Emotions like happiness, sadness, fear, rage, and surprise are hardwired and shared by everyone. Complex and frequently requiring higher-order thought, secondary emotions are not as simple as primary ones. Emotions like remorse, humiliation, and envy are examples.

Feelings are neither good nor harmful in and of themselves. Feeling cheerful, motivated, and energetic are all results of positive emotions. Depressive symptoms, anxiety, and stress are all linked to negative emotions. However, every feeling has its function. We can use emotions like fear and rage to keep us safe and assertive, respectively.

Emotional Control

Emotional well-being relies on one's capacity for responsible emotion management. Emotional intelligence is the capacity to recognize and manage our feelings constructively. Some possible approaches are listed below.

1. Finding out what causes negative feelings is the first step in dealing with them. As a result, we can learn to recognize and control our emotional reactions.

2. Mindfulness is a method of nonjudgmental attention to the present moment that should be practiced. It can aid us in recognizing and coping with our feelings without passing judgment.

3. Engage in self-affirming dialogue, which is speaking positively to oneself. It can help us deal with stressful or anxious feelings.

When feelings become too much to handle, it can be beneficial to talk to someone for support.

Seeking help from loved ones or trained professionals in mental health is crucial.

Strengthening Emotional Fortitude

"Emotional Resilience" describes a person's capacity to deal well with adversity. It enables individuals to recover quickly from setbacks and practice healthy stress management. Here are some methods that have been shown to strengthen psychological fortitude:

1. Make gratitude a regular habit; it's a potent emotion that can help you see the good in life instead of dwelling on the bad. Increasing upbeat feelings can strengthen emotional fortitude.

2. Establish Good Routines: Regular exercise, a balanced diet, and enough sleep contribute to mental well-being. They help deal and build up resistance.

3. Train yourself to have a "growth mindset," believing that one's inherent skills and talents may be honed through consistent effort. Encouraging a positive perspective in the face of adversity can aid in developing resilience.

4. Keep your attention on the here and now; doing so has been shown to lessen feelings of tension and worry. Having a hopeful outlook on life is an essential component in developing resilience.

Developing Joyful Connections with Loved Ones

Emotional health and well-being are inextricably linked to the quality of one's relationships. They're great for morale boosts and stress reduction advice. Listed below are methods that have been effective in fostering healthy relationships:

1. Communicate well by actively listening, showing emotion, and standing up for yourself. By boosting comprehension and sympathy, it can aid in developing healthy relationships.

2. Spending time with loved ones is a great way to strengthen relationships and boost morale.

3. Express gratitude and appreciation to those you care about; this will enhance your relationships and boost your mood.

4. Establish Boundaries: Boundaries are essential for maintaining good relationships. The ability to set boundaries and communicate needs and desires is necessary.

Managing Difficult Circumstances

Experiencing a significant life change like losing a loved one, getting a divorce, or losing one's career can be highly stressful. To keep one's emotions in check during these times, one must have access to reliable coping mechanisms. Some possible approaches are listed below.

1. Self-care is a practice that includes things like getting regular exercise, learning to meditate, and spending time in nature. It can aid with stress management and emotional stability.

2. Seeking support from loved ones or trained specialists in monumental health, field motion regulation, and the development of resilience in the face of adversity.

3. The ability to accept change is crucial for overcoming adversity. Getting the reality of the situation and making efforts to adjust to the shift is adaptation.

Develop your ability to bounce back from adversity through regular resilience training. Resilience is the ability to face adversity with optimism and persevere despite setbacks.

Conclusion

Physical health is nothing without mental and emotional fitness. The health of your mind and body can benefit from your efforts to learn about and control your emotions. Emotional well-being also includes developing emotional toughness and cultivating supportive relationships with others. Self-care, reaching out to others for support, and building resilience are all examples of good coping practices that can help you weather life's storms. People can improve their emotional health and progress toward a more satisfying existence by adopting these practices.

Here are ten tips for maintaining good Emotional Health

Rules of Happiness

Emotional Health

Keeping your mental and emotional health in check is crucial to your happiness and well-being. It's critical to take care of one's emotional and physical well-being. Here are some ways to keep your mind and spirit in good shape.

1. One of the best things you can do for your mental health is to get regular exercise. Stress, depression, and insomnia can all be ameliorated with a common practice.

2. Get enough sleep: Adequate sleep is crucial to maintaining mental and emotional well-being. Try to sleep for at least 7 hours nightly.

3. Maintain a healthy body and mind by eating fresh fruits and vegetables, entire grains, and lean proteins.

4. The emotional benefits of healthy relationships with loved ones and friends cannot be overstated. Hang out with upbeat, optimistic folks.

5. To maintain a healthy mental and emotional state, it's crucial to take vacations from technology every so often. Get away from screens and gadgets as much as you can.

6. Prioritize self-care by setting aside time to do things that bring you joy. Try some meditation, yoga, or writing in a journal.

7. Focus on the good things that have happened to you and thank them. Positivity and joy can result from doing this.

8. If you are having problems emotionally, it can be beneficial to speak with a therapist. A therapist can guide you and help you work through your feelings.

9. Keep your emotional health in check by establishing limits with those around you. Don't let other people walk all over you and your limits.

10. If you're feeling overwhelmed, it's crucial to reach out for assistance. Share your feelings with a therapist, close friend, or family member you trust.

If you follow these guidelines, you will better manage your emotional health. Taking care of your emotional health daily can profoundly affect your life.

Chapter 5

SOCIAL AND SPIRITUAL HEALTH AND WELL-BEING

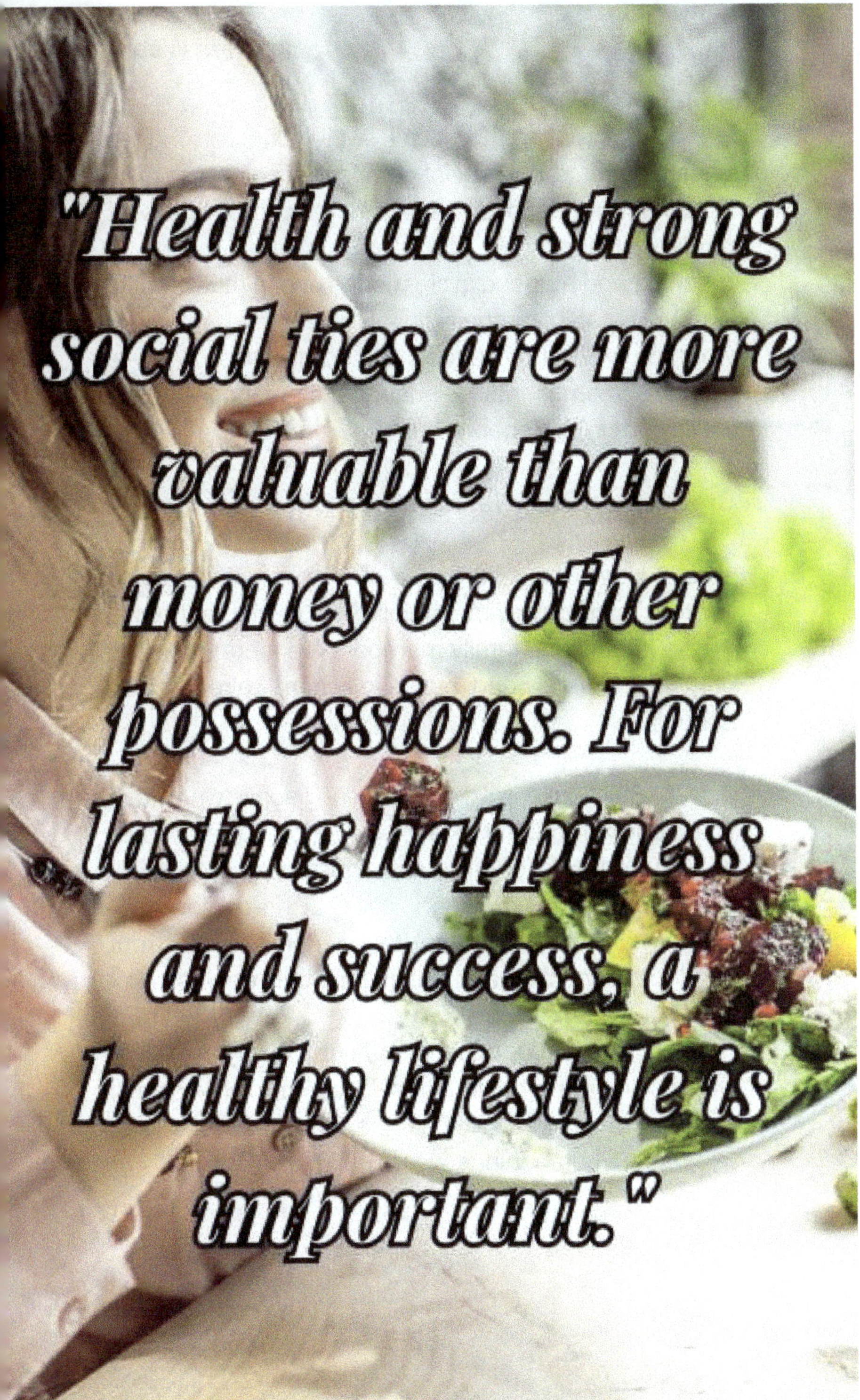

"Health and strong social ties are more valuable than money or other possessions. For lasting happiness and success, a healthy lifestyle is important."

Spiritual and social well-being are often underestimated but crucial components of health. The status of our relationships with other people indicates our social health. At the same time, our feeling of meaning and purpose in life means our spiritual health. The value of community involvement and volunteer work, as well as the effects of social media on one's mental and emotional well-being, are among the topics we'll cover in this chapter.

Creating a Safety Net for Loved Ones

Having a solid group of friends and family to lean on is crucial to maintaining good mental health. These friends and family members are there for us not only in times of need but also when we're ecstatic about life.

Building a solid network of people who have your back requires conscious effort. We should prioritize our relationships with those closest to us by setting up regular phone calls or in-person get-togethers. Asking for assistance demonstrates our need for connection and builds trust between us.

Having supportive friends and family members who inspire you to be your best is also crucial. We must surround ourselves with people who believe in and support the same things we do.

Realizing How Social Media Affects Emotional and Mental Health.

With the proliferation of social media comes the necessity of contemplating how it may affect our psychological well-being. Despite its positive effects on maintaining relationships, social media use has been linked to increased isolation, stress, and sadness.

Social media can be a source of poor self-esteem since they encourage users to compare themselves to others. When we see updates from friends traveling, getting new stuff, or having fantastic success, we may feel like we're missing out.

We must be cautious in social media usage to avoid its damaging effects on our psychological well-being. We need to be more selective about the accounts we follow and spend less time on social media overall. It's essential to check in with ourselves about social media's effects on our mental health and to step away from the screen if necessary.

Creating a More Joyful Social Life

Our social well-being depends on our ability to cultivate healthy relationships with others. Strong bonds with others help us feel like we belong and open doors to new experiences that enrich our lives.

Being a good listener and showing empathy go a long way toward building rapport with others. We must try to see things from their vantage point and acknowledge their emotions. We must admit we're wrong and accept others' apologies and forgiveness.

Good communication involves being open and courteous, avoiding making assumptions and passing judgment. We must all be willing to have tough conversations and try to find solutions that work for everyone.

The Value of Volunteering and Participating in Local Organizations

Volunteering and giving back to the community is good for our mental, emotional, and spiritual well-being. They allow us to meet new people, benefit our surroundings, and make a difference.

The mental and emotional well-being of those who volunteer also gets many rewards. It has been shown to improve mood, alleviate depression, and make people feel better about themselves and their lives.

We can find ways to serve our neighbors by contacting local nonprofits, universities, and churches. We can also join local teams or clubs that share our passions, such as sports groups or literary societies.

Important Role Of Faith In Human Health

Maintaining one's faith is crucial to one's spiritual well-being. Having faith in something bigger than yourself gives your life significance and direction. Faith is not merely an intellectual construct; it is an actuality that provides meaning and purpose to our lives.

The importance of prayer as a part of one's faith is often emphasized. Gratitude, concerns, and wants can all be sent to a higher power through prayer. People who pray regularly report excellent physical and mental health, and this practice brings them solace and calm.

A healthy spiritual life also includes the practice of forgiveness. Keeping a grudge or harboring resentment is a heavy burden to bear. Letting rid of bitterness and vengeance toward people who have harmed us is at the heart of forgiving. It's a great way to boost your emotional health, relationships, and happiness.

Spiritual restoration is also possible through repentance. To repent means to recognize personal guilt and to seek God's forgiveness. It's a way of letting go of blame and making peace with one's actions. A sense of release and a road to recovery and development can be found through genuine repentance.

Faith, prayer, forgiveness, repentance, and abandoning yourself to God are potent means to obtain God's grace and healing for one's soul. They help us feel content, fulfilled, and appreciative. We can improve our spiritual well-being and lead a more prosperous existence if we make these habits part of our everyday lives.

Conclusion

In conclusion, our happiness and well-being benefit greatly from caring for our social and spiritual health. Maintaining meaningful connections with loved ones and other people can do wonders for our emotional well-being. To protect our mental and emotional well-being, we should also limit our time spent on social media.

Here are ten tips for maintaining good Social and Spiritual Health

SOCIAL AND SPIRITUAL HEALTH

Effective communication, empathy, and listening are the cornerstones of healthy relationships. Volunteering, for example, is a meaningful activity that helps others and the larger good, which is good for our spiritual health.

In pursuing material success, we sometimes neglect the importance of caring for our emotional and mental well-being. But in today's world, it's crucial to take whatever steps are needed to maintain a healthy spiritual life. As such, I offer the following ten suggestions for keeping your spiritual and social well-being.

1. Prayer is one of the most critical steps for maintaining social and spiritual health. Through prayer, we open our hearts to the Lord, connecting with God at the deepest level. Praying daily can help us find equilibrium in our lives and bring us peace.

2. Attending Holy Mass is a great way to get in touch with God and make your faith stronger. It helps to fight spiritual apathy and brings us closer to Christ's message and other believers.

3. Confession can be very beneficial for spiritual and social health. It enables us to speak out loud about the sins that we have committed and to seek forgiveness from God.

4. Going on a retreat allows us the chance to step away from the everyday and to focus on our

relationship with God. It's an excellent opportunity to develop spiritual growth and reconnect with nature and one's faith.

5. Going on a pilgrimage is another excellent way to focus on one's spiritual growth and explore one's faith. Visiting essential sites in the Bible allows us to gain insight into our faith, as well as experience other cultures.

6. Forgiveness is essential to maintaining a healthy spiritual and social life. We must let go of grudges, forgive others, and forgive ourselves for past mistakes.

7. Patience is an invaluable tool for spiritual and social health. It's a common theme in most religions and is a vital trait to possess.

8. Kindness is essential in showing love to those around you. It's important to be open and understanding to those around us to fulfill our potential for spiritual and social health.

9. Inspired by love. Whatever action we take, it must be grounded in concern and care for those affected. We must strive to do our best for others and remain committed to our faith.

10. Finally, don't forget to take care of yourself. Self-care is essential for spiritual and social health. Take time out of your day to nurture your soul to be your best self.

Following these guidelines will aid in your emotional and social well-being. Keep in mind that serving others is a manifestation of your religion and that you are responsible for your well-being as well as the well-being of others around you.

Chapter 6

ENVIRONMENT AND HEALTH

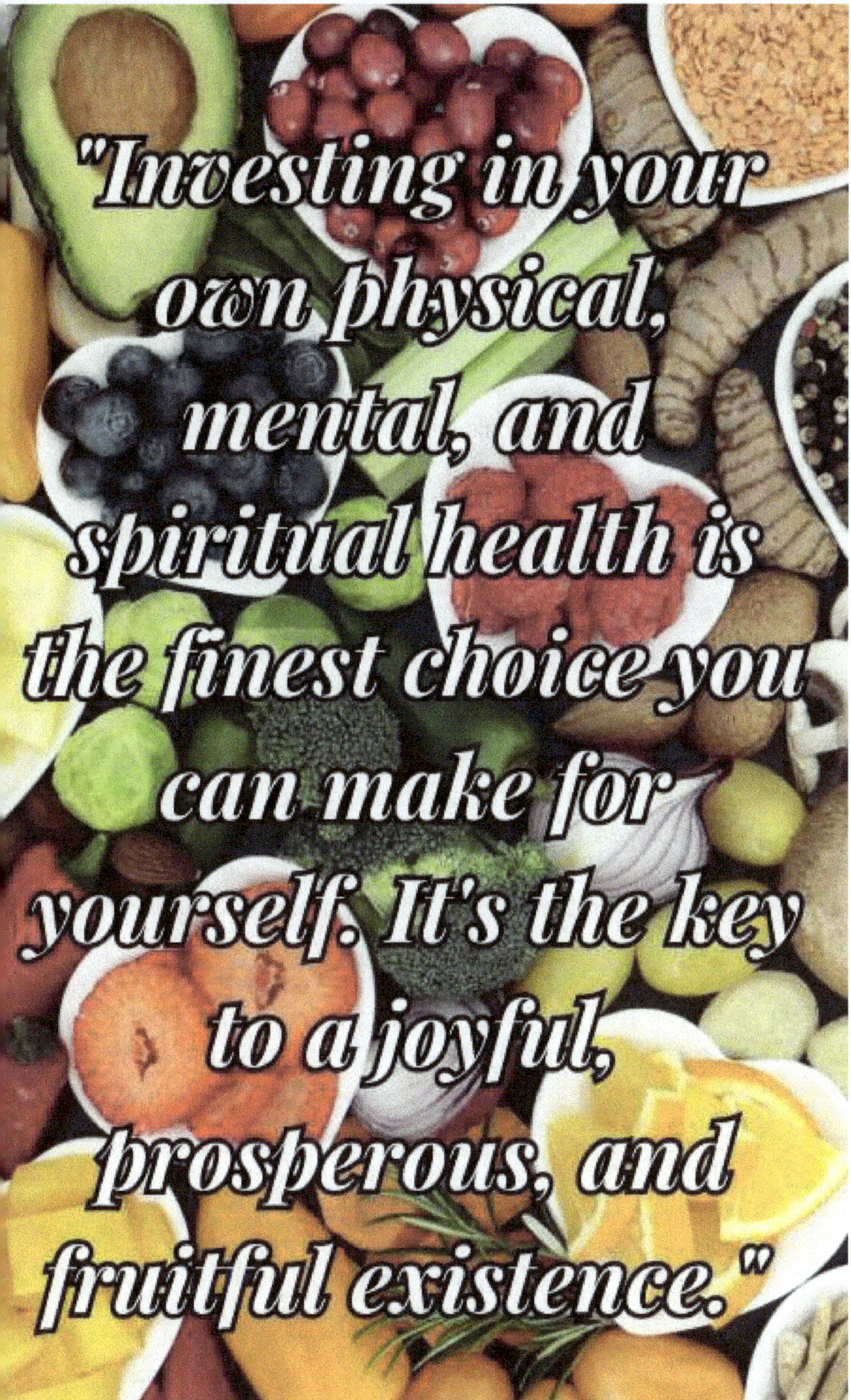

"Investing in your own physical, mental, and spiritual health is the finest choice you can make for yourself. It's the key to a joyful, prosperous, and fruitful existence."

The health effects of our surroundings are significant. Everything we come into contact with—from the air we breathe to the water we drink to the food we eat and the goods we use—impacts our health. More and more people are becoming aware of the importance of learning how our surroundings affect our health and adopting environmentally responsible practices to lessen their exposure to potentially dangerous chemicals and contaminants. In this chapter, we'll delve into these concerns and provide some helpful advice for making your home a healthier place to be.

Recognizing the significance of environmental factors in health

Many different aspects of health are affected by environmental factors. Exposure to harmful levels of sunshine and ultraviolet radiation, for instance, has been linked to cases of skin cancer. Lead and other chemicals found in polluted water have been linked to learning problems and developmental delays in children.

Therefore, it is crucial to comprehend the role the environment plays in health and to take measures to counteract the negative consequences. Alterations on both the personal and societal levels may be necessary.

Advocating for Eco-Friendly Practices

Promoting healthy, long-term lifestyle choices is one strategy to lessen the adverse effects of our environment on human health. Turning off lights and electronics when not in use, using the bus or bike, walking instead of driving, and purchasing energy-efficient equipment are all good examples of ways to cut down on energy use.

Waste reduction is another area where sustainable practices can have a significant impact. Reducing the number of times that items like straws and water bottles are used is one way to help the environment.

By changing to more eco-friendly practices, we can lessen the strain we put on the planet and protect ourselves from dangerous contaminants.

Preventative measures for air pollution and toxic chemical exposure

In addition to encouraging environmentally friendly practices, methods are available for lowering one's vulnerability to toxic chemicals and air pollution. This allows us to:

1. Many common household cleaners include chemicals that are dangerous to humans and the environment and should be avoided. It's often just as

effective and far safer to use all-natural alternatives like vinegar, baking soda, and lemon juice.

2. Try to stay away from processed foods, as they typically contain lots of unhealthy additives like artificial colors and flavors. The body may acquire the nutrients from a diet high in whole foods like fruits, vegetables, and whole grains while also reducing contact with potentially dangerous chemicals.

3. Radon is a radioactive gas that can accumulate in homes and lead to lung cancer. Therefore it's essential to have yours tested. Radon testing and mitigation are crucial preventative measures.

4. To protect yourself from lead, chlorine, and fluoride that may be present in your tap water, consider investing in a water filter. A water filter can help eliminate these harmful substances, making drinking water safer.

We can protect ourselves against harmful environmental poisons and pollutants if we know where to look for them.

Making your home a better place to live

Lastly, making your home a healthy place to live is a crucial step in protecting the environment. To do so, we must ensure the safety and well-being of the spaces in which we live and work.

Some things you can do to make your home healthier are:

1. Watch the air quality inside your home or building. Reducing exposure to dangerous pollutants can be achieved through testing indoor air quality and implementing measures to increase ventilation.

2. Use natural materials instead of those containing dangerous chemicals like formaldehyde and flame retardants, which are found in many building materials, furniture, and other products. You can reduce exposure to these pollutants by switching to natural materials like wood, cotton, and wool.

3. Maintain appropriate humidity levels to prevent the growth of mold, which can aggravate existing respiratory issues. Mold growth can be inhibited by regulating humidity through ventilation, dehumidifiers, and air conditioning.

4. Reduce your use of high-emitting products like paints, cleaners, and furniture by opting for those with lower chemical emissions. Products with third-party certifications, like GreenGuard, can help decrease exposure to these chemicals, as can using products with low emissions.

By making our homes less toxic, we can reduce our exposure to contaminants and improve our health and well-being.

Conclusion

Our health is profoundly influenced by the conditions in which we find ourselves. Protecting our health and the health of those around us requires an appreciation for the role the environment plays, the promotion of sustainable practices, and the adoption of measures to lessen exposure to poisons and pollutants. Promoting environmental health and making sure we can all thrive requires taking steps to create healthy living spaces.

Here are ten tips for maintaining and choosing a healthy environment.

ENVIRONMENT AND OUR HEALTH

Humans have a responsibility to themselves and the earth to keep the ecosystem in good condition. Here are ten guidelines for preserving a wholesome setting:

1. One of the most important things we can do to keep our planet healthy is to reduce the garbage we produce. To achieve this goal, one can recycle or repurpose anything that can be. As a result, less pollution is released into the atmosphere.

2. To further support a healthy environment, plant trees. The clean air we breathe directly results from trees releasing oxygen and sucking carbon dioxide.

3. Practice water conservation, which entails wisely using water and never letting it go to waste. The use of saltwater helps relieve pressure on potable water supplies.

4. Watch for pests: humans and animals are at risk from these unwanted visitors. Avoiding pest-infested areas and carefully checking all purchases for evidence of insects can make a big difference in maintaining a pest-free setting.

5. Cleansing product chemicals, for example, have the potential to contaminate groundwater, surface water, and the air we breathe. Chemical pollution can be mitigated through non-toxic, environmentally friendly products.

6. Loud music, construction noise, and road noise are all noise pollution that should be mitigated. Taking steps to lessen the impact of loud noises on the community is beneficial.

7. Eliminate as much trash as possible since it contains dangerous stuff like old electronics and chemicals. Garbage pollution can be reduced if these items are disposed of correctly.

8. Disease-causing organisms like anopheles mosquitoes, house flies, sewage, and other pollutants can proliferate under unsanitary conditions; thus, it is essential to maintain a healthy environment. Taking precautions to prevent or lessen exposure to these pollutants is necessary for maintaining a healthy ecosystem.

9. Promote wholesome neighborhoods by emphasizing their role in creating a setting that supports a healthy lifestyle. Safe and healthy community environments should be actively sought out and fostered.

10. To maintain a healthy ecosystem, we must limit our reliance on automobiles, which contribute to dramatic environmental issues like air pollution.

The health of humans and the world depends on our ability to keep the environment in good shape. If everyone takes these suggestions to heart, we can make the world healthier, cleaner, and less polluted.

AUTHOR'S NOTE

Health
is wealth

Health is Wealth is a practical manual that advises readers, especially those in their teens and early twenties, to put themselves first to succeed. To achieve health and wellness, the author stresses the significance of leading a healthy lifestyle and avoiding stress.

The necessity of eating a well-rounded diet is stressed throughout the book. The author stresses the need for a balanced diet of fruits, vegetables, protein, and complex carbohydrates. Obesity, diabetes, and heart disease are just some health issues resulting from a diet high in processed foods, fast food, and sugary which are discussed in detail in this book.

The author also mentions the value of water consumption in preserving health. Waste elimination, a healthy metabolic rate, and optimal organ performance depend on enough water intake. The authors suggest a daily water intake of 8-10 cups.

The value of physical activity is a prominent theme of the book as well. The book includes thorough instructions on various activities that individuals can undertake to improve their general fitness, and regular physical activity is crucial in maintaining good health. The author stresses the importance of exercise, noting its positive effects on health and happiness.

The book also looks at how stress can damage your body, mind, and spirit and offers five suggestions for dealing with it. Among these are practicing meditation, praying, sports, walking, sleeping sufficiently, and taking breaks when stressed, talking to friends or professionals, and eating healthily.

In addition, the book stresses the need for readers to take responsibility for their health and well-being by paying close attention to how they live. It emphasized the importance of taking charge of their health by scheduling regular checkups, taking medications as directed, and being immunized as necessary.

In the final chapter, the author stresses the importance of putting oneself first to succeed. It encourages people of all ages, but especially teenagers and young adults, to prioritize their health and well-being by engaging in healthy habits like regular exercise, nutritious eating, stress management, and medical attention as needed.

Finally, if you're serious about improving your health and well-being, Health Wealth is the book for you. Its insightful and actionable tips on maintaining a healthy lifestyle through nutrition, exercise, stress management, and other means are invaluable. This book is an inspiring manual for achieving a prosperous, healthy, and vital future by prioritizing self-care.

ABOUT THE AUTHOR